# Turning I

# 13 Empowerment Shifts From Impulse to Impact

K'Aelle Anthony

Turning Fire Into Fuel: 13 Empowerment Shifts From
Impulse to Impact

## Dedication

This book would not be possible if it was not for my mother, but not in a typical, momma's boy way. Jesus was a momma's boy. I may be a momma's boy but I will think about shooting you in your head and go eat dinner with the family as if nothing happened if you cross the wrong line. In my eyes she is the president, founder, CEO of turning fire into fuel! To the point where everything could be falling a part and you would never know...My brother, sister, mom, and I all once ate dinner with $5.50! Smiling, still happy, making the best out of our low point...Growing up with that strong mentality is so amazing that it has shifted my view on many things. To the point where people may think I don't care or I'm nonchalant due to the fact that I understand if it does not serve any good it does not deserve ANY of my attention and any set back is ALWAYS for a reason, a set up for the next level. Only someone who has been through countless storms could understand that fully.... My mother taught me how to trust God for the impossible. She did not give me and my siblings church. She gave us our own relationship with God. Church is surface faith, having a relationship with God is solid, deep, unshakeable faith.

# Table of Contents

# Foreword

Turning Fire Into Fuel: 13 Empowerment Shifts from Impulse to Impact is a game changer. What drives us to be better and what drives us to be bitter can be the same thing. It all comes down to choice. Our perception and reception of our experiences in life can be steppingstones or stumbling blocks. Life comes with the good, the bad, and the ugly. Taking a positive stance instead of a negative stance sets our course of life on a path of greatness. K'Aelle Anthony is my firstborn son and also the beginning of my legacy. Who he is becoming is a reflection of how he saw himself in me and the men who stood to give him a glimpse of manhood. Ultimately, he has sifted through the glimpses and found his own path to manhood. The words of wisdom in this book come from the challenges in his own life experience. While some were self-inflicted challenges others were generational inherited challenges that he is overcoming. Impulse was his middle name. Reacting and overreacting was his mode of operation. Time, failure, and growth have shifted his reactivity to responsivity. His fire for change has become his fuel to become a change agent. He chose to take lemons and make lemonade. He chose to take notes and make music. He chose to make an impulsive boy into an impactful man. The impact that he wants to make in the world has shaped and reshaped his understanding of himself as well as his understanding of the world around him. This book will change your outlook on life, your determination for your future, and your drive to become the best version of yourself.

Rev. Dr. A'Shellarien Lang, A.A., B.S., MDiv, STM, ThD
CEO of Desakajo's Flo

# Introduction

Have you ever wondered why you feel out of control sometimes? What makes you lose your temper in one situation but not in another? The more you tell yourself that you will maintain your composure the more you seem to lose it. Impulse is the driving force for many men whether they know it or not. In this world we live in today, black men are being killed for impulsively standing up for what is right. Even though that sounds like an oxymoron, it has been the case since slavery. Black men were "tamed" during slavery by the slave owner to minimize his impulse to be free. The Willie Lynch letter of 1712, whether authentic or not, helps make the point of how black men were "tamed":

**I HAVE A FULL PROOF METHOD FOR CONTROLLING YOUR BLACK SLAVES**. I guarantee every one of you that, if installed correctly, **IT WILL CONTROL THE SLAVES FOR AT LEAST 300 HUNDREDS YEARS**. My method is simple. Any member of your family or your overseer can use it. **I HAVE OUTLINED A NUMBER OF DIFFERENCES AMONG THE SLAVES; AND I TAKE THESE DIFFERENCES AND MAKE THEM BIGGER. I USE FEAR, DISTRUST AND ENVY FOR CONTROL PURPOSES**. These methods have worked on my modest plantation in the West Indies and it will work throughout the South. Take this simple little list of differences and think about them. On top of my list is "AGE," but it's there only because it starts with an "a." The second is "COLOR" or shade. There is **INTELLIGENCE, SIZE, SEX, SIZES OF PLANTATIONS, STATUS** on plantations, **ATTITUDE** of owners, whether the slaves live in the valley, on a hill, East, West, North, South, have fine hair, course hair, or is tall or short. Now that you have a list of differences, I shall give you an outline of action, but before that, I shall assure you that **DISTRUST IS STRONGER THAN TRUST AND ENVY STRONGER THAN ADULATION, RESPECT OR ADMIRATION**. The Black slaves after receiving this indoctrination shall carry on and will become self-refueling and self-generating for **HUNDREDS** of years, maybe **THOUSANDS**. Don't forget, you must pitch the **OLD** black male vs. the **YOUNG** black male, and the **YOUNG** black male against the **OLD** black male. You must use the **DARK** skin slaves vs. the **LIGHT** skin slaves, and the **LIGHT** skin slaves vs. the **DARK** skin slaves. You must use the **FEMALE** vs. the **MALE**, and the **MALE** vs. the **FEMALE**. You must also have white servants and overseers [who] distrust all Blacks. But it is **NECESSARY THAT YOUR SLAVES TRUST AND DEPEND ON US. THEY MUST LOVE, RESPECT AND TRUST ONLY US**. Gentlemen, these kits are your keys to control. Use them. Have your wives and children use them, never miss an opportunity. **IF USED INTENSELY FOR ONE YEAR, THE SLAVES THEMSELVES WILL REMAIN PERPETUALLY DISTRUSTFUL**. Thank you gentlemen."

For orderly future, special and particular attention must be paid to the **FEMALE** and the **YOUNGEST** offspring. Both must be **CROSSBRED** to produce a variety and division of labor. Both must be taught to respond to a peculiar new **LANGUAGE**. Psychological and physical instruction of **CONTAINMENT** must be created for both. We hold the six cardinal principles as truth to be self-evident, based upon following the discourse concerning the economics of breaking and tying the horse and the nigger together, all inclusive of the six principles laid down above. NOTE: Neither principle alone will suffice for good economics. All principles must be employed for orderly good of the nation. Accordingly, both a wild horse and a wild or natur[al] nigger is dangerous even if captured, for they will have the tendency to seek their customary freedom and, in doing so, might kill you in your sleep. You cannot rest. They sleep while you are awake, and are awake while you are asleep.

They are **DANGEROUS** near the family house and it requires too much labor to watch them away from the house. Above all, you cannot get them to work in this natural state. Hence, both the horse and the nigger must be broken; that is breaking them from one form of mental life to another. **KEEP THE BODY, TAKE THE MIND!** In other words, break the will to resist. Now the breaking process is the same for both the horse and the nigger, only slightly varying in degrees. But, as we said before, there is an art in long range economic planning. **YOU MUST KEEP YOUR EYE AND THOUGHTS ON THE FEMALE and the OFFSPRING** of the horse and the nigger. A brief discourse in offspring development will shed light on the key to sound economic principles. Pay little attention to the generation of original breaking, but **CONCENTRATE ON FUTURE GENERATION**. Therefore, if you break the **FEMALE** mother, she will **BREAK** the offspring in its early years of development; and when the offspring is old enough to work, she will deliver it up to you, for her normal female protective tendencies will have been lost in the original breaking process. When it comes to breaking the uncivilized nigger, use the same process, but vary the degree and step up the pressure, so as to do a complete reversal of the mind. Take the meanest and most restless nigger, strip him of his clothes in front of the remaining male niggers, the female, and the nigger infant, tar and feather him, tie each leg to a different horse faced in opposite directions, set him afire and beat both horses to pull him apart in front of the remaining niggers. The next step is to take a bullwhip and beat the remaining nigger males to the point of death, in front of the female and the infant. Don't kill him, but **PUT THE FEAR OF GOD IN HIM**, for he can be useful for future breeding.

**THE BREAKING PROCESS OF THE AFRICAN WOMAN**

Take the female and run a series of tests on her to see if she will submit to your desires willingly. Test her in every way, because she is the most important factor for good economics. If she shows any sign of resistance in submitting completely to your will, do not hesitate to use the bullwhip on her to extract that last bit of [b----] out of her. Take care not to kill her, for in doing so, you spoil good economics. When in complete submission, she will train her offsprings in the early years to submit to labor when they become of age. Understanding is the best thing. Therefore, we shall go deeper into this area of the subject matter concerning what we have produced here in this breaking process of the female nigger. We have reversed the relationship; in her natural uncivilized state, she would have a strong dependency on the uncivilized nigger male, and she would have a limited protective tendency toward her independent male offspring and would raise male offsprings to be dependent like her. Nature had provided for this type of balance. We reversed nature by burning and pulling a civilized nigger apart and bullwhipping the other to the point of death, all in her presence. By her being left alone, unprotected, with the **MALE IMAGE DESTROYED**, the ordeal caused her to move from her psychologically dependent state to a frozen, independent state. In this frozen, psychological state of independence, she will raise

11

her **MALE** and female offspring in reversed roles. For **FEAR** of the young male's life, she will psychologically train him to be **MENTALLY WEAK** and **DEPENDENT**, but **PHYSICALLY STRONG**. Because she has become psychologically independent, she will train her **FEMALE** offsprings to be psychologically independent. What have you got? You've got the nigger **WOMAN OUT FRONT AND THE** nigger **MAN BEHIND AND SCARED**. This is a perfect situation of sound sleep and economics. Before the breaking process, we had to be alertly on guard at all times. Now, we can sleep soundly, for out of frozen fear his woman stands guard for us. He cannot get past her early slave-molding process. He is a good tool, now ready to be tied to the horse at a tender age. By the time a nigger boy reaches the age of sixteen, he is soundly broken in and ready for a long life of sound and efficient work and the reproduction of a unit of good labor force. Continually through the breaking of uncivilized savage niggers, by throwing the nigger female savage into a frozen psychological state of independence, by killing the protective male image, and by creating a submissive dependent mind of the nigger male slave, we have created an orbiting cycle that turns on its own axis forever, unless a phenomenon occurs and re-shifts the position of the male and female slaves. We show what we mean by example. Take the case of the two economic slave units and examine them close.

Earlier, we talked about the non-economic good of the horse and the nigger in their wild or natural state; we talked out the principle of breaking and tying them together for orderly production. Furthermore, we talked about paying particular attention to the female savage and her offspring for orderly future planning, then more recently we stated that, by reversing the positions of the male and female savages, we created an orbiting cycle that turns on its own axis forever unless a phenomenon occurred and reshifts positions of the male and female savages. Our experts warned us about the possibility of this phenomenon occurring, for they say that the mind has a strong drive to correct and re-correct itself over a period of time if it can touch some substantial original historical base; and they advised us that the best way to deal with the phenomenon is to shave off the brute's mental history and create a multiplicity of phenomena of illusions, so that each illusion will twirl in its own orbit, something similar to floating balls in a vacuum. This creation of multiplicity of phenomena of illusions entails the principle of crossbreeding the nigger and the horse as we stated above, the purpose of which is to create a diversified division of labor; thereby creating different levels of labor and different values of illusion at each connecting level of labor. The results of which is the severance of the points of original beginnings for each sphere illusion. Since we feel that the subject matter may get more complicated as we proceed in laying down our economic plan concerning the purpose, reason and effect of crossbreeding horses and niggers, we shall lay down the following definition terms for future generations. Orbiting cycle means a thing turning in a given path. Axis means upon which or around which a body turns. Phenomenon means something beyond ordinary conception and inspires awe and wonder. Multiplicity means a great number. Means a globe. Crossbreeding a horse means taking a horse and breeding it with an ass and you get a dumb, backward, ass long-headed mule that is not reproductive nor productive by itself. Crossbreeding niggers mean taking so many drops of good white blood and putting them into as many nigger women as possible, varying the drops by the various tone that you want, and then letting them breed with each other until another circle of color appears as you desire. What this means is this: Put the niggers and the horse in a breeding pot, mix some asses and some good white blood and what do you get? You got a multiplicity of colors of ass backward, unusual niggers, running, tied to backward ass long-headed mules, the one productive of itself, the other sterile. (The one constant, the other dying, we keep the nigger constant for we may replace the mules for another tool) both mule and nigger tied to each other, neither knowing where the other came from and neither productive for itself, nor without each other.

The "taming" process that black men went through was a devastating blow to the black culture spiritually as well as naturally. Black men went from being acculturated to be physically strong and mentally weak through the breaking process of chattel slavery to institutionalized compliance through mass incarceration. The methodology was the same while the presented reason was said to be different. The "fear" of the black man remains evident and embedded in the foundational fabric of our societal construct. The impulse to be a free man with his own sense of worth was controlled yet never erased from the hearts and minds of men then, or now.

Impulse in and of itself is not bad. Impulse is a sudden spontaneous inclination. In other words it is an instinctive force to do something immediately like our flight or fight instinct. Impulse is not bad in all situations. A man's impulse to provide for himself and his family is good. A man's impulse to protect himself is good, unless it is in the presence of someone trying to oppress him. The impulse to move from boyhood to manhood is good.

What is manhood? Who determines what it means to be a man? Manhood in one culture looks very different in another culture. Manhood in one faith tradition looks very different in another faith tradition. Manhood would seem to be a noun yet it has the makings of a verb. As a noun, it is a state of being. A place you arrive in your life's journey. As a verb, it is something that is constantly changing and moving. It is something that grows as you grow. It is ever changing spaces in the life of a man. While the dictionary declares that manhood is a noun, it seems more appropriate to say that it is a verb. Manhood is relative to the male that is experiencing it. To say that one has arrived at manhood is to say that one has reached a level of male perfection.

Reaching true manhood is an ongoing, ever-changing, and challenging experience for men. Change can be good. Change can be bad. Our perception of change is what drives the impulse to resist the change or the impact that comes with embracing the change. Manhood is something to attain yet it is also something to fight against. The social construct of manhood has altered the desire for some men to achieve the presented manhood of the day. Manhood is defined within the contextual understanding of the men who ultimately shape boys. To say that one is a man has been skewed by men and women telling boys, "You are the man of the house now." What does that really mean? How would a boy know what it means to be a man? How can they successfully achieve manhood without a clear example of what that looks like or sounds like?

Manhood is something you grow into. The evolution from boyhood to manhood comes with some challenges that cannot be overlooked. Impulsivity is a life altering hurdle that boyhood fosters while manhood tames. Impulsivity is displaying behavior in reaction to something without thinking about it first. The saying, "Boys will be boys" fosters the impulsivity in boys and makes it the norm. Unfortunately, that same saying is used for men who have not overcome their reactionary approach to life. Reacting to situations in life takes the discipline out of the equation. Reacting, being impulsive, does not require any thought. There is no active engagement with intentional thinking. Impulsivity is a recipe for disaster for the simple fact that reacting instead of responding leads to destruction. Destruction can result in emotional and physical collateral damage. All those who get hurt in the process of reactionary behavior become collateral damage. There are some people, relationships, and lives that never recover from other peoples' reactionary behavior. A perfect example of physical collateral damage would be driving recklessly because you are angry. Impulse to soothe your anger is now the driving force and you wind up killing somebody in the process. Your distracted driving has the death of an innocent person as its collateral damage. An example of emotional collateral damage would be using your negative love experience to drive how you teach your son how to be in relationships. You display negative manhood traits like yelling at his mother, disrespecting her with other women, and dishonoring her by choosing not to be a good man. Your choice to have a negative impact leaves your broken son as emotional collateral damage.

Reacting is when there is no space for thought between the activating event and the behavior displayed in the given situation. Responding on the other hand is when there is space for thought between the activating event and the behavior displayed in the given situation. Responding in situations is a sign of maturity, a sign of discipline, a sign of wanting to have positive impact. Positive impact is the fruit of Manhood, the verb. Impulsivity, reacting, is not the standard. Responding, impact, is the standard. Impact is the effect that you have on something or someone. Unfortunately, impact is a two-edged sword. There can be positive impact as well as negative impact. Being male does not automatically mean that you will achieve the positive state of manhood. The shift from boyhood to manhood never happens for some men. Some men remain in the unfruitful stage of development that does not allow them to mature. Some boys are not raised in an environment conducive to seeing and learning from a man who is achieving positive manhood. As stated earlier, negative images also have an impact. It is in the determination of the boy that dictates what he gleans from the men around him. Manhood is relative to the men displaying it.

Manhood, the verb, has spiritual and natural components. The natural component of manhood can is fired up by foolishness. The spiritual component of manhood is fueled by faith. Achieving manhood from a natural perspective tames impulsivity. Achieving manhood from a spiritual perspective aims to have a positive impact on the boys that are being cultivated. Anger seems to be the catalyst that unleashes impulse or impact. How men choose to use their anger determines their destiny. If one chooses to use the fire of anger, the impulse, the flames can easily become out of control. If one chooses to use the fuel of anger, impact, the flames of the same fire will have order. Ralph Marston said, "You've done it before and you can do it now. See the positive possibilities. Redirect the substantial energy of your frustration and turn it into positive, effective, unstoppable determination." Marston helps us understand that the choice to take the negative path is always available. However, the better choice is to take the energy and redirect it towards something positive. The Bible says in Psalm 37:23 (AMP), "The steps of a [good and righteous] man are directed *and* established by the LORD, And He delights in his way [and blesses his path]." It also says in 1 Corinthians 13:11-12 (AMP), "When I was a child, I talked like a child, I thought like a child, I reasoned like a child; when I became a man, I did away with childish things. For now [in this time of imperfection] we see in a mirror dimly [a blurred reflection, a riddle, an enigma], but then [when the time of perfection comes we will see reality] face to face. Now I know in part [just in fragments], but then I will know fully, just as I have been fully known [by God]." The Bible has many stories of men who transition from boyhood to manhood. For the purposes of showing the movement from boyhood impulse to manhood impact, let us look at Joseph's story.

There is a story in the Bible about a young man named Joseph. Joseph was the son of Rachael and Jacob. Rachael was the beloved wife of Jacob. Jacob met and fell in love with Rachael and agreed to work for her father, Laban, to have her as his wife. Jacob worked for 7 years to marry Rachael. On their wedding night her father tricked him and gave him Rachael's older sister Leah as his wife. The next morning he confronted his father in law. Jacob eventually conceded to remain married to Leah and marry Rachael, the one he truly loved, with the understanding that he would have to work another 7 years. After 7 days, Laban gave him Rachael to be his wife as well. Rachael could not have children while Leah gave birth to 6 sons and 1 daughter. When Rachael did conceive she gave birth to Joseph. Joseph was beloved by his father because he loved his mother so much. Jacob fostered hatred for Joseph among his other sons because he favored Joseph. While Joseph was special, he was also impulsive and had no humility. He would go out into the fields with his brothers and come back and tell his father all that they did. He was a dreamer and shared his dreams with his brother and father. His dreams had his family serving him. Unfortunately, while they were prophetic, they also stirred the anger that his brothers already had against him. In reaction to Joseph's impulsive behavior that taunted his brothers, his brothers sold him to the Ishmaelites who in turn sold him to Potiphar in Egypt.

God was with Joseph even in his times of distress. He found favor with Potiphar and rose to a high position in leadership. Joseph was very attractive and eventually Potiphar's wife wanted Joseph. When Joseph rejected her, she accused him of raping her and Potiphar threw him in prison. God was with Joseph in prison and he rose to a high position of leadership. He interpreted dreams in prison that led to him being released form prison after interpreting the

King's dream. Again, God was with Joseph and he rose to a high position of leadership. He became second in command as Egypt went through 7 prosperous years and 7 years of famine.

Joseph found favor with God and the Egyptians during the 7 prosperous years. He married and had two sons. In the beginning of the 7 years of famine Joseph's brothers came before him to buy grain. They did not recognize Joseph even though Joseph recognized them. Joseph devised a plot to toy with them because his impulse to torment them was real and he wanted to see his younger brother Benjamin. Eventually the scam played out and Joseph came clean with his brothers. He reunited with his father and the rest of their family. Joseph resisted the urge to continue to torment is brothers because he knew that God was using him to impact many lives. God had set him up to be able to take care of his family. Joseph's life is a good example of moving from impulsive boyhood to impactful manhood.

As we look at Joseph's life, we can see that experience was his greatest teacher. Even in the midst of his boyhood impulsivity, God was the driving force for his ultimate impact. As he grew into manhood there were moments where he wrestled between impulse and impact. The frustration that Marston talked about is evident in many challenging times Joseph experienced in his life. There are so many nuggets that can be gleaned from Joseph's story. This book will use Joseph's story to share thirteen empowerment shifts from impact to impulse. Why empowerment? Why shift? Empowerment because it invokes a necessary movement from who you are to who you are becoming. It creates the space to cultivate the best of you to become the better you. Shift because you must replace the uninformed you with who God has called you to be. You are exchanging that which was to that which is. Empowerment shift because the better you is changing places with the uniformed you.

Manhood, the verb, can be seen through the lens of thirteen empowerment shifts: Faith; Focus; Fertile;

--

Foundation; Favor; Fervent; Fruitful; Fervour; Flow; Freedom; Failure; Feelings; and Fulfill. The faith lens displays what undergirds the entirety of manhood. The focus lens displays the direction to manhood. The fertile lens displays the groundwork for manhood. The foundation lens displays the proper seeds sown for manhood. The favor lens displays God's hand in manhood. The fervent lens displays the strong beliefs in manhood. The fruitful lens cultivates the seeds of manhood. The fervour lens displays the passionate drive in manhood. The flow lens displays the intentional maneuvering in manhood. The freedom lens displays the truth in manhood. The failure lens displays the stumbling blocks in manhood. The feelings lens displays the emotions in manhood. Finally, the fulfill lens displays the destiny in manhood.

This book that you hold in your hands will bring a fresh natural and spiritual perspective to what it means to move through the twists and turns of manhood. Each empowerment shift has a G.E.A.R. (Giving Everything A Response) at the end. The G.E.A.R. is designed to give you the practiced discipline to resist impulse (reaction) and engage each empowerment shift by answering three questions (response): What is your reality? What is your reflection? What is your responsibility? The three questions will draw you into a conversation with Joseph's story as his life answers those same three questions. As you explore your journey to and through manhood with these 13 empowerment shift lenses, allow your truth to shape and reshape your voice about who you are becoming as well as your vision for where you will be going.

# G.E.A.R.
## Giving Everything A Response

## Who Am I Becoming?

**Joseph's Reality-** He was the beloved first child of a mother who was loved yet broken and thought she would never have children. He was beloved of his father because he loved his mother and hated by his brothers for that very reason. He was taught how to be a man by a father who loved and served God, loved his family, yet facilitated anger among his children because he impulsively catered to Joseph.

**My Reality:**_____
_____
_____
_____

**Joseph's Reflection-** He loved God more than his anger toward his brothers. In his pursuit of God, he had to let go of his vendetta against those who hurt him. He had to rise above his hurt and anger so that God could use him to be a blessing to the masses.

**My Reflection:**_____
_____
_____
_____

**Joseph's Responsibility-** It is more important to do the right thing in love than to be right in anger. The choice to extend grace and walk in integrity must be intentional.

**My Responsibility:**_____
_____
_____
_____

# Chapter One

## Empowerment Shift #1
## FAITH

*A man is the master gardener of his soul, the director of his life.*

What does faith have to do with manhood? Why does it matter what I believe? Manhood is going to move whether I include God or not, why should I care? Faith is defined as the complete trust or confidence in someone or something. The ebb and flow of manhood comes with challenges. It is not easy to navigate the complexities of manhood alone. Faith is that which undergirds the entirety of the journey through manhood in a positive impactful way. Faith is empowerment shift #1. Living your faith in God gives the journey direction, balance, and destination. Direction deals with hearing, balance deals with feeling, and destination deals with thinking.

Building a relationship with God will foster the ability to hear God's direction. Hearing does not have to be an audible conversation with God's thunderous voice like in the movies. Hearing God happens in a song, in a scripture, in words of wisdom from someone you least expect it from, as well as, a still small voice that sounds just like you. Hearing God only happens when you yield your spirit to God's spirit. Faith will allow you to trust God more than you trust yourself. Allowing God's direction in your life will usher in the balance that you need in your life. Managing your emotions is equivalent to allowing God to bring balance in your life. Emotions can take you on a roller coaster ride that is out of control. Making space for God to bring you emotional balance will allow you to grab your impulse to react right in its tracks and make it subject to God's direction. Finally, your thought process is directly connected to yielding to God's direction, which gives you emotional balance, which ultimately will give you the mental agility to remain on course to your true destination. Mental agility is the ability to have situational awareness and sound judgement in the moment. Mental agility with faith is the ability to have spiritual situational awareness in the midst of making the decision to react or to respond. Your destination is yours to decide. How you think leads to how you feel which leads to what you do.

God has a plan for your life. Your thought process about

what God has designed for you will make or break you

reaching your true destination. Faith matters. Having faith in

God matters.

Let's look at Joseph's story as we continue to explore

the empowerment shift of faith. Genesis 37:1-8 begins

Joseph's story:

> Joseph, *being* seventeen years old, was feeding the
> flock with his brothers. And the lad *was* with the sons
> of Bilhah and the sons of Zilpah, his father's wives;
> and Joseph brought a bad report of them to his father.
> ³ Now Israel loved Joseph more than all his children,
> because he *was* the son of his old age. Also he made
> him a tunic of *many* colors. ⁴ But when his brothers
> saw that their father loved him more than all his
> brothers, they hated him and could not speak
> peaceably to him. ⁵ Now Joseph had a dream, and he
> told *it* to his brothers; and they hated him even
> more. ⁶ So he said to them, "Please hear this dream
> which I have dreamed: ⁷ There we were, binding
> sheaves in the field. Then behold, my sheaf arose
> and also stood upright; and indeed your sheaves
> stood all around and bowed down to my sheaf." ⁸ And
> his brothers said to him, "Shall you indeed reign over
> us? Or shall you indeed have dominion over us?" So
> they hated him even more for his dreams and for his
> words.

Joseph was an impulsive teenager who underestimated his brothers' hatred for him. He was accustomed to having his way at the expense of his brothers. His faith in God did not move him to have compassion on his brothers. He was still growing into manhood. His faith was still being shaped by his impulse to torment his brothers. While God was still with him, God gave him space to make his own faith choices. What faith choices are you making? What space is God giving you right now?

# G.E.A.R.
## Giving Everything A Response

## Who Am I Becoming? FAITH

**Joseph's Reality**-Joseph used his God given gift as a way to torment his brothers. His brothers hated him and he fed that anger. His faith took a back seat to his fleshly desire.

**My Reality**:_____
_____
_____
_____

**Joseph's Reflection**- Joseph pushed his brothers to a point where they could not even talk to him. Joseph's choice to put flesh over faith dishonored God, his brothers, and himself.

**My Reflection**:_____
_____
_____
_____

**Joseph's Responsibility**- It is more important to do the right thing in love than to be right in anger. The choice to extend grace and walk in integrity must be intentional.

**My Responsibility**:_____
_____
_____
_____

# Chapter Two

## Empowerment Shift #2
## FOCUS

*Thought and character are one, character can only manifest and discover itself through environment and circumstance.*

Where is your focus? What do you spend the majority of your time thinking about, planning, and doing? Focus is that which commands the majority of your attention. Focus is what gives the direction in the movement through manhood. Focus is empowerment shift #2. The direction you choose to go must line up with the direction that God wants for your life. What you spend your time thinking about will eventually manifest in your character. There is miscommunication about the link between what we think and what we do. While there is a school of thought that says there is no correlation, science has taught us that what you think leads to how you feel which leads to what you do. Whatever you mentally concentrate on will show up somewhere. If you think about a negative love experience most of your day, your focus will be on love not working out. Your behavior that evening will display a negative image of love in a relationship. Suppose you meet a woman that night, will she get the neutral you or will she get the negative love experience you? Your impulse to see her through the lens of every woman who hurt you will be the fire that directs you. Taking the time to be intentional about what you focus on would give you opportunity to give this new woman a clean slate. The impact of the clean slate could be the best relationship that you have ever had.

Who you are becoming is directly reflected in your character. Your character is a direct reflection of your thought process. As you grow into the man God called you to be, your environment plays a major role in how you are shaped. You choose your direction not the circumstances your are forced to endure. Let life be your training ground. There is always something to learn from every experience. You either learn what you should do or what you should not do. When you see your circumstances in life as learning opportunities your frustration will me minimized. That is not to say that your focus will not be off sometimes. Life happens. We all get distracted by various things in life. Your chosen direction must in alignment with God. Your ability to say yes to God and mean yes to God is what will keep you focused through the good times and the bad times.

Let's look at Joseph's story in Genesis 37:9-10 as we continue to explore the empowerment shift of focus:

> [9] Then he dreamed still another dream and told it to his brothers, and said, "Look, I have dreamed another dream. And this time, the sun, the moon, and the eleven stars bowed down to me." [10] So he told *it* to his father and his brothers; and his father rebuked him and said to him, "What *is* this dream that you have dreamed? Shall your mother and I and your brothers indeed come to bow down to the earth before you?" [11] And his brothers envied him, but his father kept the matter *in mind*.

Joseph was so eager to tell his dream that he lost his focus. God did not intend for Joseph to make his father and brothers feel bad. Everything God gives us is not meant to be spoken to the people in the dream. It takes intentionality to follow God's direction and maintain our good character. In Joseph's excitement, he did not think about how his dream would be received and perceived by his family. Focus gives direction in manhood. Unlike the GPS, you do not have to give a play by play of where God is taking you. The choice is yours to honor God or not? Your character is a direct reflection of who you believe God to be. You represent God in thought, word, and deed. What direction have you chosen?

# G.E.A.R.
## Giving Everything A Response

## Who Am I Becoming?

**Joseph's Reality**- Joseph was a dreamer. Joseph was a man who heard from God. Joseph was a man who was learning how to be a man.

**My Reality**:_____

_____

_____

_____

**Joseph's Reflection**- Joseph allowed his excitement about what God showed him to alter his family's perception of his character. His thoughts about what he saw were not filtered in kindness for his family which led to them seeing him in a bad light.

**My Reflection**:_____

_____

_____

_____

**Joseph's Responsibility**- It is more important to do the right thing in love than to be right in anger. The choice to extend grace and walk in integrity must be intentional.

**My Responsibility**:_____

_____

_____

_____

# Chapter Three

## Empowerment Shift #3
## FERTILE

*Good thought bares good fruit, bad thoughts bares bad fruit.*

What consumes your thoughts? If you had to rate

yourself on a scale of 1 to 10: Ten being good thoughts most

of the time and 1 being bad thoughts most of the time, where

would you say you are? Thoughts become your words. Your

words turn into action. Your action becomes the fruit of your

mind. Your mind is fertile in that you can plant good seeds or

bad seeds. Your fertile mind lays the groundwork as you

move through manhood. Fertile is empowerment shift #3.

What is in your head will eventually come to your lips.

What is on your lips will eventually produce the good or bad

fruit of your actions. You have the final say in what you allow

to be planted in the fertile ground of your mind. Sometimes

we allow the frustrations of life to consume us. When we

look at the frustration through the lens of fire, it gets us

stirred up and ready to take action in a negative way to bring about the change we seek. If we take that same frustration and look at it through the lens of fuel, we can formulate a plan of action in the fertile ground of our mind and become a change agent. There is a lot more than can be done with responsive planned effort than spontaneous reaction. How do we get to the place where we slow down long enough to even consider whether our groundwork is being fertilized in a good way or bad way? Use God as the barometer to decide what kind of planting is going on. If your thought dishonors God, it will produce bad fruit. If your thought honors God, it will produce good fruit. Moving from impulse to impact has a lot to do with how much honoring God matters to you.

Let's look at Joseph's story in Genesis 37:12-36 and 39:1-6 as we continue to explore the empowerment shift of fertile:

> 12 Then his brothers went to feed their father's flock in Shechem. 13 And Israel said to Joseph, "Are not your brothers feeding *the flock* in Shechem? Come, I will send you to them." So he said to him, "Here I am." 14 Then he said to him, "Please go and see if it is well with your brothers and well with the flocks, and bring back word to me." So he sent him out of the Valley of Hebron, and he went to Shechem. 15 Now a certain man found him, and there he was, wandering in the

field. And the man asked him, saying, "What are you seeking?" ¹⁶ So he said, "I am seeking my brothers. Please tell me where they are feeding *their flocks.*" ¹⁷ And the man said, "They have departed from here, for I heard them say, 'Let us go to Dothan.' " So Joseph went after his brothers and found them in Dothan.¹⁸ Now when they saw him afar off, even before he came near them, they conspired against him to kill him. ¹⁹ Then they said to one another, "Look, this dreamer is coming! ²⁰ Come therefore, let us now kill him and cast him into some pit; and we shall say, 'Some wild beast has devoured him.' We shall see what will become of his dreams!"²¹ But Reuben heard *it,* and he delivered him out of their hands, and said, "Let us not kill him." ²² And Reuben said to them, "Shed no blood, *but* cast him into this pit which *is* in the wilderness, and do not lay a hand on him"—that he might deliver him out of their hands, and bring him back to his father.²³ So it came to pass, when Joseph had come to his brothers, that they stripped Joseph *of* his tunic, the tunic of *many* colors that *was* on him. ²⁴ Then they took him and cast him into a pit. And the pit *was* empty; *there was* no water in it.²⁵ And they sat down to eat a meal. Then they lifted their eyes and looked, and there was a company of Ishmaelites, coming from Gilead with their camels, bearing spices, balm, and myrrh, on their way to carry *them* down to Egypt. ²⁶ So Judah said to his brothers, "What profit *is there* if we kill our brother and conceal his blood? ²⁷ Come and let us sell him to the Ishmaelites, and let not our hand be upon him, for he *is* our brother and our flesh." And his brothers listened. ²⁸ Then Midianite traders passed by; so *the brothers* pulled Joseph up and lifted him out of the pit, and sold him to the Ishmaelites for twenty *shekels* of silver. And they took Joseph to Egypt.²⁹ Then Reuben returned to the pit, and indeed Joseph *was* not in the pit; and he tore his clothes. ³⁰ And he returned to his brothers and said, "The lad *is* no *more;* and I, where shall I go?"³¹ So they took Joseph's tunic, killed a kid of the goats, and dipped the tunic in the blood. <sup>32</sup> Then they sent the tunic of *many* colors, and they brought *it* to their father and said, "We have found this. Do you know whether it *is* your son's tunic or not?"<sup>33</sup> And he recognized it and said, "*It is* my son's tunic. A wild beast has devoured him. Without doubt Joseph is torn to pieces." <sup>34</sup> Then Jacob tore his clothes, put sackcloth on his waist, and mourned for his son many days. <sup>35</sup> And all his sons and all his daughters arose to comfort him; but he refused to be comforted, and he said, "For I shall go down into the grave to my son in mourning." Thus his father wept for him.<sup>36</sup> Now the Midianites had sold him in Egypt to Potiphar, an officer of Pharaoh *and* captain of the guard

Now Joseph had been taken down to Egypt. And Potiphar, an officer of Pharaoh, captain of the guard, an Egyptian, bought him from the Ishmaelites who had taken him down there. <sup>2</sup> The LORD was with Joseph, and he was a successful man; and he was in the house of his master the Egyptian.
<sup>3</sup> And his master saw that the LORD *was* with him and that the LORD made all he did to prosper in his hand. <sup>4</sup> So Joseph found favor in his sight and served him. Then he made him overseer of his house, and all *that* he had he put under his authority. <sup>5</sup> So it was, from the time *that* he had made him overseer of his house and all that he had, that the LORD blessed the Egyptian's house for Joseph's sake; and the blessing of the LORD was on all that he had in the house and in the field. <sup>6</sup> Thus he left all that he had in Joseph's hand, and he did not know what he had except for the bread which he ate.

What we see is that Joseph's mind was fertile ground for God to get the glory. Joseph could have allowed the frustration of being left in a pit and sold by his brothers to consume him. He could have allowed the frustration of going from the beloved, privileged, favorite son of his father to being sold as a slave in Egypt saturate his mind in a negative way. From the story we see that Joseph chose to allow good thoughts to be the groundwork of his move through manhood. It is clear that he understood God was moving without liking how God was moving. Even in the midst of a bad situation, Joseph chose to trust God. The fertile ground of his mind was saturated with good thoughts that honored God. The fruit of his actions produced God's favor in his life. He did not have to force it. Potiphar, his master, recognized it on his own. As you move through manhood, what are you allowing to saturate the fertile ground of your mind? Is it honoring God or dishonoring God?

# G.E.A.R.
## Giving Everything A Response

## Who Am I Becoming? FERTILE

**Joseph's Reality**- Joseph was in a very frustrating space of manhood. He was hurt, angry, disappointed. He did not see this in his dreams. He had a major decision to make, allow good thoughts to shape his character or allow bad thoughts to shape his character.

**My Reality**:_____
_____
_____
_____

**Joseph's Reflection**- Joseph made the choice to allow the fertile ground of his mind to be saturated with good thoughts to produce good fruit. His choice to honor God brought him to a place of favor.

**My Reflection**:_____
_____
_____
_____

**Joseph's Responsibility**- It is more important to do the right thing in love than to be right in anger. The choice to extend grace and walk in integrity must be intentional.

**My Responsibility**:_____
_____
_____
_____

# Chapter Four

## Empowerment Shift #4
## FOUNDATION

*Circumstance does not make a man, it reveals a man.*

What is your manhood built upon? What principles or values do you hold near and dear? You can have the best looking structure, however without a firm foundation, it will fall. Your foundation is that which provides the proper nutrients and cultivation environment for the seeds of greatness that you sow along your journey from boyhood to manhood. Foundation is empowerment shift #4. Seeds are interesting in that they must be buried in order to grow.

Seeds are so small yet have the ability to create such enormous impact. Each seed is destined to be a specific thing. It is in the process of being buried in a firm foundation that the seed begins to become what it is destined to be. Manhood has the same process. The burying process, the hidden places that God allows you to be, shapes you in ways that you may never completely understand. Unfortunately, the impulse to be unburied and free keeps men from the necessary process of germination. Germination is the process of growth for a seed. Who you are becoming must be germinated in a firm foundation of God's values and principles. What looks good to you is not always good for you. What it looks like on the outside may be very different than what it is truly like on the inside. As you grow into manhood, how you react or respond to various circumstances will reveal who you are becoming as a man. The seeds that you sow, whether good seeds or bad seeds, will blossom. It is your choice to cultivate your seeds with God's word, worship, and study. Honoring God enhances your foundation. It makes it ripe and ready for the good seeds that you choose to be fertilized.

A proper foundation built on God's principles will undoubtedly take you from impulse to impact. Let's look at Joseph's story in Genesis 37:6-23 as we continue to explore the empowerment shift of foundation:

> Now Joseph was handsome in form and appearance.
> [7] And it came to pass after these things that his master's wife cast longing eyes on Joseph, and she said, "Lie with me." [8] But he refused and said to his

master's wife, "Look, my master does not know what *is* with me in the house, and he has committed all that he has to my hand. **9** *There is* no one greater in this house than I, nor has he kept back anything from me but you, because you *are* his wife. How then can I do this great wickedness, and sin against God?"**10** So it was, as she spoke to Joseph day by day, that he did not heed her, to lie with her *or* to be with her.**11** But it happened about this time, when Joseph went into the house to do his work, and none of the men of the house *was* inside, **12** that she caught him by his garment, saying, "Lie with me." But he left his garment in her hand and fled and ran outside. **13** And so it was, when she saw that he had left his garment in her hand and fled outside, **14** that she called to the men of her house and spoke to them, saying, "See, he has brought in to us a Hebrew to mock us. He came in to me to lie with me, and I cried out with a loud voice. **15** And it happened, when he heard that I lifted my voice and cried out, that he left his garment with me, and fled and went outside."**16** So she kept his garment with her until his master came home. **17** Then she spoke to him with words like these, saying, "The Hebrew servant whom you brought to us came in to me to mock me; **18** so it happened, as I lifted my voice and cried out, that he left his garment with me and fled outside."**19** So it was, when his master heard the words which his wife spoke to him, saying, "Your servant did to me after this manner," that his anger was aroused. **20** Then Joseph's master took him and put him into the prison, a place where the king's prisoners *were* confined. And he was there in the prison. **21** But the LORD was with Joseph and showed him mercy, and He gave him favor in the sight of the keeper of the prison. **22** And the keeper of the prison committed to Joseph's hand all the prisoners who *were* in the prison; whatever they did there, it was his doing. **23** The keeper of the prison did not look into anything *that was under*

*Joseph's* authority, because the LORD was with him; and whatever he did, the LORD made *it* prosper.

Joseph had a firm foundation in God. He was not moved by what he saw, how he felt, or what he was experiencing. His trust was completely in God. He was literally buried in a prison that he did not deserve to be in. The seed of greatness on the inside of him was completely saturated in the nutrients of God. The circumstance of his present did not hinder who God was shaping him to be for his future. What are your seeds saturated in? Is your foundation built upon God?

# G.E.A.R.
## Giving Everything A Response

## Who Am I Becoming? FOUNDATION

**Joseph's Reality**- Joseph was experiencing a germination process that was quite painful. He was imprisoned for doing the right thing. His foundation was solid yet his circumstance was shaky.

**My Reality**:_____

_____

_____

_____

**Joseph's Reflection**- Joseph made the choice to allow God's germination process to shape him into a man of impact. He resisted the impulse to resist the burying process. His seed of greatness required a very frustrating circumstance. His true character of being a man after God's heart was revealed in the process.

**My Reflection**:_____

_____

_____

_____

**Joseph's Responsibility**- It is more important to do the right thing in love than to be right in anger. The choice to extend grace and walk in integrity must be intentional.

**My Responsibility**:_____

_____

_____

_____

# Chapter Five

## Empowerment Shift #5
## FAVOR

*Men do not attract what they say that want, they attract who they are.*

What do you want for your life? Who do you attract in your life? Take a minute to look closer at the patterns in your life, what is drawn to you and what are you drawn to? It will undoubtedly change the way you see yourself if you knew who was really watching you. Oftentimes people use us as virtual mentors based on what they perceive to be God's favor on our lives. God's unmerited hand over your life, orchestrating your moves, defying what the adversary had planned for you, created spaces and graces that you clearly could never have done yourself is favor. Favor is empowerment shift #5. When we yield our spirit to God's spirit, amazing things happen. Doors open, windows open, doors close and windows close.

While having favor on your life if amazing, it is also challenging. What favor brings into your life is life changing. What favor takes out of your life is life changing as well. As you move through the ebb and flow of manhood, favor is in place to add as well as to subtract. There are spaces that favor will allow you to be and there are spaces that favor will not allow you to be. The bible says in Psalm 23, "Grace and mercy shall follow me all the days of my life." Well with that being the case, your yes to God does not come with you getting to decide what that yes entails. There are certain places that grace and mercy will need to go to through you that you will have no choice but to get to. Having favor on your life is not about you nor is it for you. When you say yes to God, what you want becomes secondary to who God has called you to be to the people that God has sent to you and sends you to. Your ability to stay in spiritual communication with God, prayer and at times fasting, will show you who is in your life for a reason, a season, and a lifetime.

The reason people will recognize your favor and use you to get from point A to point B. Your presence in their life is brief yet feeds their impulse to change their lives. The season people will recognize your favor and walk with you temporarily to get what they need from you. Your presence in their lives is temporary yet impactful. Finally, the lifetime people will recognize your favor and leave what they thought was life to become a mentee. Your presence in their lives is ongoing as long as you remain clear about the impact that you are supposed to have in their lives. Sometimes we get the 3 mixed up based on our desire to help God out. We get attached to people in ways that cloud our judgement. Prayer and fasting is a must as you continue to walk in God's favor.

The favor on your life attracts two kinds of people: Those who honor the spirit of God in you and those who make it their life's work to dishonor and devalue the spirit of God in you. Your attention to detail, your resistance to react to the reason, season, and lifetime experience, and your desire to move in the spirit of impact will determine how the favor of God on your life continues. Let's look at Joseph's story in Genesis 40 as we continue to explore the empowerment shift of favor:

> It came to pass after these things *that* the butler and the baker of the king of Egypt offended their lord, the king of Egypt. [2] And Pharaoh was angry with his two officers, the chief butler and the chief baker. [3] So he

put them in custody in the house of the captain of the guard, in the prison, the place where Joseph was confined. <sup>4</sup> And the captain of the guard charged Joseph with them, and he served them; so they were in custody for a while.<sup>5</sup> Then the butler and the baker of the king of Egypt, who *were* confined in the prison, had a dream, both of them, each man's dream in one night *and* each man's dream with its own interpretation. <sup>6</sup> And Joseph came in to them in the morning and looked at them, and saw that they were sad. <sup>7</sup> So he asked Pharaoh's officers who *were* with him in the custody of his lord's house, saying, "Why do you look *so* sad today?" <sup>8</sup> And they said to him, "We each have had a dream, and *there is* no interpreter of it." So Joseph said to them, "Do not interpretations belong to God? Tell *them* to me, please."

<sup>9</sup> Then the chief butler told his dream to Joseph, and said to him, "Behold, in my dream a vine *was* before me, <sup>10</sup> and in the vine *were* three branches; it *was* as though it budded, its blossoms shot forth, and its clusters brought forth ripe grapes. <sup>11</sup> Then Pharaoh's cup *was* in my hand; and I took the grapes and pressed them into Pharaoh's cup, and placed the cup in Pharaoh's hand."<sup>12</sup> And Joseph said to him, "This *is* the interpretation of it: The three branches *are* three days. <sup>13</sup> Now within three days Pharaoh will lift up your head and restore you to your place, and you will put Pharaoh's cup in his hand according to the former manner, when you were his butler. <sup>14</sup> But remember me when it is well with you, and please show kindness to me; make mention of me to Pharaoh and get me out of this house. <sup>15</sup> For indeed I was stolen away from the land of the Hebrews; and also I have done nothing here that they should put me into the dungeon."

16 When the chief baker saw that the interpretation was good, he said to Joseph, "I also *was* in my dream, and there were three white baskets on my head. 17 In the uppermost basket *were* all kinds of baked goods for Pharaoh, and the birds ate them out of the basket on my head." 18 So Joseph answered and said, "This *is* the interpretation of it: The three baskets *are* three days. 19 Within three days Pharaoh will lift off your head from you and hang you on a tree; and the birds will eat your flesh from you." 20 Now it came to pass on the third day, *which was* Pharaoh's birthday, that he made a feast for all his servants; and he lifted up the head of the chief butler and of the chief baker among his servants. 21 Then he restored the chief butler to his butlership again, and he placed the cup in Pharaoh's hand. 22 But he hanged the chief baker, as Joseph had interpreted to them. 23 Yet the chief butler did not remember Joseph, but forgot him.

Joseph had God's favor on his life, yet he was in some very challenging situations. The favor made him beloved and the favorite child of his father, yet he was hated by his brothers. Favor allowed him to dream prophetically, yet those same dreams cost him his life with his family. Hatred brought him to Egypt, yet favor sustained him. Lies brought him to jail, yet favor sustained him. The leader that he was born to be kept creating space for him regardless of the challenging situation he found himself in. Joseph's desire to honor God allowed him to recognize the favor on his own life. He understood that the favor on his life was not about him, even though it hurt going through the process. The people attracted to him were sent because of who he was called by God to be. In your life, who are you called to be? Have you yielded to God's call on your life to be a leader? What does the favor of God look like in your life?

## G.E.A.R.
## Giving Everything A Response

## Who Am I Becoming? FAVOR

**Joseph's Reality**- Joseph was in jail for something he did not do. He chose to allow the favor on his life to order his steps even though the place where he found himself was unfair.

**My Reality**:_____

_____

_____

_____

**Joseph's Reflection**- Joseph's yes to God was not contingent upon the good places and spaces where he found himself. Favor is not fair in that it creates good spaces and challenging spaces for the one favored and the one getting the benefits of the favored.

**My Reflection**:_____

_____

_____

_____

**Joseph's Responsibility**- It is more important to do the right thing in love than to be right in anger. The choice to extend grace and walk in integrity must be intentional.

**My Responsibility**:_____

_____

_____

_____

# Chapter Six

## Empowerment Shift #6
## FERVENT

*A man will not get what he wishes and prays for apart from what he justly earns. His wishes and prayers are only gratified and answered when they are in alignment with his good thoughts and actions.*

What are your strong beliefs about manhood? What are your standards of excellence? What will you not settle for? Manhood, the verb, requires intentionality. It requires a fervent, strong belief, allegiance to values and principles that are uncompromising. Fervent is empowerment shift #6. In the face of very difficult situations, being fervent will keep you on the path that God has laid out for you.

There are times when your move from boyhood to manhood will require you to dig your heels in and be fervent in your stance of what it means to be a man. You may pray and wish for one thing while God has something entirely different in the works for you. What you spend time planning and preparing for will hold much more value to you in the end. Getting what you did not earn loses its value over time.

Putting the time and energy into your growth and development will ultimately take you from impulse to impact in a way that changes your life and the lives of those around you. Your life is on display when you say yes to God. Your move toward fervent allegiance to what God says about what makes a good man, keeps you in alignment with God's plan for your life. Who you are becoming must reflect your intentionality to be a man after God's heart. Your pursuit of God must never be contingent upon you getting what you want more than God getting what God wants.

Your thoughts and actions can take you places you want to go as well as places you do not want to go. Your ability to manage you is the key that unlocks the door to your greatness. Let's look at Joseph's story in Genesis 41:1-36 as we continue to explore the empowerment shift of fervent:

> Then it came to pass, at the end of two full years, that Pharaoh had a dream; and behold, he stood by the river. ² Suddenly there came up out of the river seven cows, fine looking and fat; and they fed in the meadow. ³ Then behold, seven other cows came up after them out of the river, ugly and gaunt, and stood by the *other* cows on the bank of the river. ⁴ And the ugly and gaunt cows ate up the seven fine looking

and fat cows. So Pharaoh awoke. ⁵ He slept and dreamed a second time; and suddenly seven heads of grain came up on one stalk, plump and good. ⁶ Then behold, seven thin heads, blighted by the east wind, sprang up after them. ⁷ And the seven thin heads devoured the seven plump and full heads. So Pharaoh awoke, and indeed, *it was* a dream.⁸ Now it came to pass in the morning that his spirit was troubled, and he sent and called for all the magicians of Egypt and all its wise men. And Pharaoh told them his dreams, but *there was* no one who could interpret them for Pharaoh.⁹ Then the chief butler spoke to Pharaoh, saying: "I remember my faults this day. ¹⁰ When Pharaoh was angry with his servants, and put me in custody in the house of the captain of the guard, *both* me and the chief baker, ¹¹ we each had a dream in one night, he and I. Each of us dreamed according to the interpretation of his *own* dream. ¹² Now there *was* a young Hebrew man with us there, a servant of the captain of the guard. And we told him, and he interpreted our dreams for us; to each man he interpreted according to his *own* dream. ¹³ And it came to pass, just as he interpreted for us, so it happened. He restored me to my office, and he hanged him."¹⁴ Then Pharaoh sent and called Joseph, and they brought him quickly out of the dungeon; and he shaved, changed his clothing, and came to Pharaoh. ¹⁵ And Pharaoh said to Joseph, "I have had a dream, and *there is* no one who can interpret it. But I have heard it said of you *that* you can understand a dream, to interpret it."¹⁶ So Joseph answered Pharaoh, saying, "*It is* not in me; God will give Pharaoh an answer of peace."¹⁷ Then Pharaoh said to Joseph: "Behold, in my dream I stood on the bank of the river. ¹⁸ Suddenly seven cows came up out of the river, fine looking and fat; and they fed in the meadow. ¹⁹ Then behold, seven other cows came up after them, poor and very ugly and gaunt, such ugliness as I have never seen in all the land of

Egypt. **20** And the gaunt and ugly cows ate up the first seven, the fat cows. **21** When they had eaten them up, no one would have known that they had eaten them, for they *were* just as ugly as at the beginning. So I awoke. **22** Also I saw in my dream, and suddenly seven heads came up on one stalk, full and good. **23** Then behold, seven heads, withered, thin, *and* blighted by the east wind, sprang up after them. **24** And the thin heads devoured the seven good heads. So I told *this* to the magicians, but *there was* no one who could explain *it* to me."**25** Then Joseph said to Pharaoh, "The dreams of Pharaoh *are* one; God has shown Pharaoh what He *is* about to do: **26** The seven good cows *are* seven years, and the seven good heads *are* seven years; the dreams *are* one. **27** And the seven thin and ugly cows which came up after them *are* seven years, and the seven empty heads blighted by the east wind are seven years of famine. **28** This *is* the thing which I have spoken to Pharaoh. God has shown Pharaoh what He *is* about to do. **29** Indeed seven years of great plenty will come throughout all the land of Egypt; **30** but after them seven years of famine will arise, and all the plenty will be forgotten in the land of Egypt; and the famine will deplete the land. **31** So the plenty will not be known in the land because of the famine following, for it *will be* very severe. **32** And the dream was repeated to Pharaoh twice because the thing *is* established by God, and God will shortly bring it to pass.**33** "Now therefore, let Pharaoh select a discerning and wise man, and set him over the land of Egypt. **34** Let Pharaoh do *this,* and let him appoint officers over the land, to collect one-fifth *of the produce* of the land of Egypt in the seven plentiful years. **35** And let them gather all the food of those good years that are coming, and store up grain under the authority of Pharaoh, and let them keep food in the cities. **36** Then that food shall be as a reserve for the land for the seven years of famine which shall be in the land of Egypt, that the land may not perish during the famine."

Joseph had a fervent, strong belief, allegiance to who God called him to be. He could have used this opportunity before the Pharaoh to sing his woes about the horrible hand that he had been dealt. He could have used this opportunity to bargain with Pharaoh for his release before he did what God had designed for him to do all along. Joseph most assuredly was praying for God to release him from prison, change his circumstances, and restore him to the life that he was accustomed to. Joseph could have reacted, been impulsive, in his desire for justice in that moment. Instead, Joseph decided to respond. He chose to resist his impulse to get what he was wishing and praying for in the moment so that God could use him in a powerful way. In the end, what Joseph wished and prayed for was answered after his words and actions aligned with God's plan for his life. He put the time in and earned his right to be called a man after God's heart.

Joseph's words and actions were aligned with God. God knew that Joseph could be trusted with this particular assignment. God has a specific assignment for you, are you prepared to hold fast to what God says is a good man? Will you be able to resist your impulse to be vindicated so that God will be able to use you to have a major impact on people, places, and things?

# G.E.A.R.
## Giving Everything A Response

## Who Am I Becoming? FERVENT

**Joseph's Reality**- Joseph chose to allow God to get the glory out his life. His fervent allegiance to who God called him to be as he journey through manhood required that he deny himself at times.

**My Reality**:_____
_____
_____
_____

**Joseph's Reflection**-Joseph's choice to move away from impulse allowed him to be a blessing to people who forgot about him initially. Eventually, Joseph's impact was received by the highest authority in the land. God's timing always plays a part in what we want and pray for.

**My Reflection**:_____
_____
_____
_____

**Joseph's Responsibility**- It is more important to do the right thing in love than to be right in anger. The choice to extend grace and walk in integrity must be intentional.

**My Responsibility**:_____
_____
_____
_____

## Chapter Seven

## Empowerment Shift #7
## FRUITFUL

*In the long run, good thoughts and actions can never produce bad results.*

What are you producing in your life? Do your thoughts and actions line up with your intentions? Are you actively engaged in your growth and development? Are you pursing those who sow seeds of greatness into you? Fruitful is that space on the journey of manhood where you are intentional about the seeds that are sown into your life as well as the seeds you sow into the lives of others. Fruitful is empowerment shift #7. Being good fruit and bearing good fruit is a product of moving from impulse to impact.

Good fruit comes from good trees. Bad fruit comes from bad trees. A good tree cannot produce bad fruit and vice versa. What you sow into you is going to come out of you. Sowing seeds of discord, anger, bitterness, laziness, and anything that is contrary to who God called you to be as a man will absolutely manifest as the product of who you are choosing to be. Sowing seeds of love, kindness, leadership, integrity, honor, valor, and the like will absolutely manifest a great harvest as you grow into who you are becoming. Fruit must be cultivated to be its best. The seed is chosen very carefully, the place where it is buried is chosen very carefully, and the conditions in which it grows it chosen very carefully. Your thoughts and actions are the product of the seeds that you have allowed to be sown into you.

It must be your intention to monitor the seeds that you sow into your spirit. What you watch, who you allow to be in your space, what you feed your spirit, they all matter. God wants to use good fruit. While it is true that we see that God uses bad fruit, however that use is temporary. As you learn how God wants to use you, you will develop clearer discernment about who comes to sow good seed or bad seed. Everyone who is with you is not for you. You are the one who must decipher who gets access to you or not. Every fruit must be handled in accordance to their ability to handle pressure. A peach must be handled gently because it bruises easily. A red delicious apple can be handled differently because it can handle a different amount of

pressure. Only you and God know what you can handle.

Let's look at Joseph's story in Genesis 41:37-45 as we

continue to explore the empowerment shift of fruitful:

> [37] So the advice was good in the eyes of Pharaoh and in the eyes of all his servants. [38] And Pharaoh said to his servants, "Can we find *such a one* as this, a man in whom *is* the Spirit of God?"[39] Then Pharaoh said to Joseph, "Inasmuch as God has shown you all this, *there is* no one as discerning and wise as you. [40] You shall be over my house, and all my people shall be ruled according to your word; only in regard to the throne will I be greater than you." [41] And Pharaoh said to Joseph, "See, I have set you over all the land of Egypt."[42] Then Pharaoh took his signet ring off his hand and put it on Joseph's hand; and he clothed him in garments of fine linen and put a gold chain around his neck. [43] And he had him ride in the second chariot which he had; and they cried out before him, "Bow the knee!" So he set him over all the land of Egypt. [44] Pharaoh also said to Joseph, "I *am* Pharaoh, and without your consent no man may lift his hand or foot in all the land of Egypt."[45] And Pharaoh called Joseph's name Zaphnath Paaneah and he gave him as a wife Asenath, the daughter of Poti-Pherah priest of On. So Joseph went out over *all* the land of Egypt.

Joseph was good fruit that God could use and trust.

Joseph could have allowed his frustrations to become bad

fruit that altered who God had called him to be. The seeds of his bad thoughts could have changed the course of his life in a way that he may have never recovered from. He chose to hold onto the good seeds that God had sown into him as God used him to sow good seeds in the Pharaoh. What are you allowing to be sown in your life? Have you taken authority over your life in that you are the doorkeeper of your life who manages the seeds that come in and the seeds that go out?

# G.E.A.R.
## Giving Everything A Response

## Who Am I Becoming? FRUITFUL

**Joseph's Reality**- Joseph had a rough life after he was sold by his brothers. It was trial after trial, yet his thoughts and actions remained connected to God's call on his life which made him good fruit. Although his dream said he would rule, his life experience had him serving.

**My Reality**:_____

_____

_____

_____

**Joseph's Reflection**- Joseph's insistence on holding on to the seeds of good thoughts and actions made him good fruit. The product of his good thoughts and actions was God using him to bless a nation.

**My Reflection**:_____

_____

_____

_____

**Joseph's Responsibility**- It is more important to do the right thing in love than to be right in anger. The choice to extend grace and walk in integrity must be intentional.

**My Responsibility**:_____

_____

_____

_____

# Chapter Eight

## Empowerment Shift #8
## FERVOUR

*Happiness, health, and prosperity are the results of a harmonious adjustment of balance between the inner and outer aspects of the man and his surroundings. A man only begins to be a man when he ceases to whine and revile and commences to search for a hidden justice which regulates his life. As he adapts his mind to that regulating factor, he ceases to accuse others as the cause of his condition. He builds himself up in strong and noble thoughts and uses that as means of discovering the hidden powers and possibilities within himself.*

What drives you? What matters to you? What are you pursuing in your life? Something is driving you from boyhood to manhood. Something is telling you who you are becoming. Fervour is the passionate drive that moves you from one place in your life to another. Fervour is empowerment shift #8. That which drives you passionately will set the pace for how you move through the ebb and flow of manhood.

The things that matter you, matter to God. Your happiness, your health, and your prosperity are topics of discussion in the Bible. How you balance your inner being and your outer being are also topics of discussion in the Bible. What you have on the inside is directly reflected on the outside. Who we see is only the manifestation of the inner work that you have been doing. Who and what you hold accountable for your success or failure is up to you. Ultimately, fervour, your passionate drive, regulates how you manage yourself along the way. It can not be someone else's fault, your environment, your lack of resources, no male role model, or anything else that drives you. Your fervour must be rooted and grounded in who God is for you.

The balance that you find in your life is yours. No one can claim ownership of your choices. You regulate you. Your thoughts and actions are a direct reflection of the choices you make in your life. It is true that we can be the collateral damage of other people's choices. It is also true that we are the deciding factor of where we end up. Your fervour to be who God called you to be reveals the hidden powers and possibilities that have been in you from your mother's womb. Let's look at Joseph's story in Gensis 41:46-51 as we continue to explore the empowerment shift of fervour:

⁴⁶ Joseph was thirty years old when he stood before Pharaoh king of Egypt. And Joseph went out from the presence of Pharaoh and went throughout all the land of Egypt. ⁴⁷ Now in the seven plentiful years the ground brought forth abundantly. ⁴⁸ So he gathered up all the food of the seven years which were in the land of Egypt, and laid up the food in the cities; he laid up in every city the food of the fields which surrounded them. ⁴⁹ Joseph gathered very much grain, as the sand of the sea, until he stopped counting, for *it was* immeasurable. ⁵⁰ And to Joseph were born two sons before the years of famine came, whom Asenath the daughter of Poti-Pherah priest of On, bore to him. ⁵¹ Joseph called the name of the firstborn Manasseh: "For God has made me forget all my toil and all my father's house." ⁵² And the name of the second he called Ephraim: "For God has caused me to be fruitful in the land of my affliction."

Joseph struggled for 23 years. He was 17 when he was thrown in a pit and sold to Potiphar in Egypt. There were more challenging days within those 23 years than he cared for. Yet he made the choice to allow fervour for God to settle into his heart and mind during the good times as well as the bad times. Joseph went from being a prisoner to second in command over all of Egypt. God needed to be able to trust Joseph to remain faithful while he wielded all that power. Fervour is a passionate drive. It can be a good drive or a bad drive. Passion can have a mind of its own when left to itself.

You have the inner power to control the outer manifestation of who you are becoming. It is that inner power that must be connected to God. Your connection to God will shape how your passion comes to fruition. Joseph understood that God had a plan even though the way the plan was unfolding was very frustrating. In the midst of your frustration, have you chosen to honor God like Joseph did? Does your inner man have balance with your outer man? Can God trust you?

# G.E.A.R.
## Giving Everything A Response

## Who Am I Becoming? FERVOUR

**Joseph's Reality**- The struggle was real for Joseph. It took every bit of the spirit of God in him to manage himself in the midst of his hardest times. He made the choice to honor God.

**My Reality**:_____

_____

_____

_____

**Joseph's Reflection**- Joseph knew what he knew yet it was still hard. To know that God is with you and to live as God is with you are two very different things. Joseph made the choice to balance his inner man with his outer man.

**My Reflection**:_____

_____

_____

_____

**Joseph's Responsibility**- It is more important to do the right thing in love than to be right in anger. The choice to extend grace and walk in integrity must be intentional.

**My Responsibility**:_____

_____

_____

_____

## Chapter Nine

## Empowerment Shift #9
## FLOW

*Men imagine that their thoughts can be kept secret. They cannot.
They rapidly crystallize into habit and habit solidifies into
circumstances. A man cannot directly choose his circumstances,
but he can choose his thoughts and so indirectly can shape how he
perceives his circumstances.*

What do your thoughts reveal about who you are? Do you see the glass as half full or half empty? Over the course of your journey from boyhood to manhood, struggle will occur. Circumstances beyond your control will change the course of your life. The flow, your ability to intentionally maneuver as God leads you, in your life must reflect your surrender to God's will for your life. Flow is empowerment shift #9. God has a plan and a purpose for you. It is up to you to listen to God's instructions.

Your thoughts lead to how you feel which leads to what you do. There is nothing hidden from God. What you think eventually manifests in your actions. If you think something long enough, it will become a habit. A habit is something that you do without even thinking about it. Serving God must be intentional. How you serve God must be intentional. Your choices have a consequence. Consequences come with circumstances. Some circumstances are welcomed and some are not. Whether your choice is to honor God or dishonor God, circumstances will follow. Your decision to honor God's flow for your life will make your journey more bearable. There will be times when the punishment does not fit the crime. In those times, God can still get the glory out of your life. God gives you the directions for how your intentional maneuver will go. It won't always be pleasant, however, it will be a way that God uses you.

Your thought process around what God is doing in your life will allow for smooth flow or impede the flow. Either way the flow is moving. Either you will fall in line and follow the intentional maneuver God gives you or God will use someone else who will. Let's look at Joseph's story in Genesis 41:53-57 as we continue to explore the empowerment shift of flow:

**53** Then the seven years of plenty which were in the land of Egypt ended, **54** and the seven years of famine began to come, as Joseph had said. The famine was in all lands, but in all the land of Egypt there was bread. **55** So when all the land of Egypt was famished, the people cried to Pharaoh for bread. Then Pharaoh said to all the Egyptians, "Go to Joseph; whatever he says to you, do." **56** The famine was over all the face of the earth, and Joseph opened all the storehouses and sold to the Egyptians. And the famine became severe in the land of Egypt. **57** So all countries came to Joseph in Egypt to buy *grain,* because the famine was severe in all lands.

Joseph made the choice to surrender his thoughts to God. The circumstances he found himself in were unimaginable at times. He went from the best to the worst to the best to the worst back to the best. In the midst of the back and forth, he was alone. He was snatched away from his family and had to learn to fend for himself. His negative thoughts were not hidden from God. His pain was not hidden from God. His desire to be loved was not hidden from God.

Joseph knew that God had a flow for his life even though it came with some painful experiences. Joseph had no say in how his life played out. He did have a choice to listen to the instructions that God gave him. The intentional maneuvering that Joseph had in his life would not work for everyone. What God does in your life is contextualized for you. Your thoughts around how moves in your life is your choice. Perception is reality. What are you saying to yourself about how God desires you to flow in and through you? Have you completely surrendered your will to God's will so that your flow will not be impeded?

## G.E.A.R.
### Giving Everything A Response

### Who Am I Becoming? FLOW

**Joseph's Reality**- Joseph was surrendered to God. He understood that his thought and his actions were a direct reflection of who God was in his life and who God was trying to be in the lives of the Egyptians.
**My Reality**:_____
_____
_____
_____

**Joseph's Reflection**- Joseph had to be honest with God and trust that God's plan for his life would eventually work out for his good. His good thoughts outweighed his bad thoughts. God was able to get the glory even in the tough times.
**My Reflection**:_____
_____
_____
_____

**Joseph's Responsibility**- It is more important to do the right thing in love than to be right in anger. The choice to extend grace and walk in integrity must be intentional.

**My Responsibility**:_____
_____
_____
_____

# Chapter Ten

## Empowerment Shift #10
## FREEDOM

*Thought, purpose, and achievement. Until thought is linked with purpose there is no true achievement.*

What do you imagine yourself being in the future? As you look back over your life what still holds you hostage to the hurt in your life? Your struggle to get to a better place in your life did not come without tears. Hurt is painful. Life comes with pain. What you think about that hurt determines how you come through it. Freedom is your ability to embrace the truths in your life as you move from boyhood to manhood. Freedom is empowerment shift #10. Your freedom is inextricably linked to who God is in your life and God's truth about who you are.

Life happens to us all. There are good days and bad days. Joyful moments and sad moments happen for all of us. There are times when you feel defeated and lost. There are times when you feel on top of the world. Your thoughts lay the framework for how you will embrace or reject your purpose. Circumstances in life can feel like jail. Your reliance on God for guidance will give you the keys to what feels like jail. You feel restricted and inhibited from being all that you desire to be. Your purpose in life nudges you to leave that jail to pursue those things you wish to accomplish in life. How you think about your purpose either nudges you out into the deep or causes you to hide in the jail because it seems safer.

When your thoughts line up with your purpose you will achieve what God has planned for your life. It is hard to achieve what you cannot conceive. Being stuck in a place of hurt based on what has happened in your past is a perfect example of embracing a lie instead of the truth. The truth about manhood is that you are an overcomer. What does not kill you will ultimately make you stronger. Let's look at Joseph's story in Genesis 42:6-24 as we continue to explore the empowerment shift of freedom:

> Now Joseph *was* governor over the land; and it was he who sold to all the people of the land. And

Joseph's brothers came and bowed down before him with *their* faces to the earth. <sup>7</sup> Joseph saw his brothers and recognized them, but he acted as a stranger to them and spoke roughly to them. Then he said to them, "Where do you come from?" And they said, "From the land of Canaan to buy food."<sup>8</sup> So Joseph recognized his brothers, but they did not recognize him. <sup>9</sup> Then Joseph remembered the dreams which he had dreamed about them, and said to them, "You *are* spies! You have come to see the nakedness of the land!"<sup>10</sup> And they said to him, "No, my lord, but your servants have come to buy food. <sup>11</sup> We *are* all one man's sons; we are honest men; your servants are not spies."<sup>12</sup> But he said to them, "No, but you have come to see the nakedness of the land."<sup>13</sup> And they said, "Your servants *are* twelve brothers, the sons of one man in the land of Canaan; and in fact, the youngest *is* with our father today, and one *is* no more." <sup>14</sup> But Joseph said to them, "It *is* as I spoke to you, saying, 'You *are* spies!' <sup>15</sup> In this *manner* you shall be tested: By the life of Pharaoh, you shall not leave this place unless your youngest brother comes here. <sup>16</sup> Send one of you, and let him bring your brother; and you shall be kept in prison, that your words may be tested to see whether *there is* any truth in you; or else, by the life of Pharaoh, surely you *are* spies!" <sup>17</sup> So he put them all together in prison three days.<sup>18</sup> Then Joseph said to them the third day, "Do this and live, *for* I fear God: <sup>19</sup> If you are honest *men,* let one of your brothers be confined to your prison house; but you, go and carry grain for the famine of your houses. <sup>20</sup> And bring your youngest brother to me; so your words will be verified, and you shall not die." And they did so. <sup>21</sup> Then they said to one another, "We *are* truly guilty concerning our brother, for we saw the anguish of his soul when he pleaded with us, and we would not hear; therefore this distress has come upon us."<sup>22</sup> And Reuben answered them, saying, "Did I not speak to you, saying, 'Do not sin against the boy'; and you would not listen? Therefore behold, his blood is now required of us." **23** But they did not know that Joseph understood *them,* for he spoke to them through an interpreter. **24** And he turned himself away from them and wept. Then he returned to them again and talked with them. And he took Simeon from them and bound him before their eyes.

Joseph was held hostage to his hurt. The truth about his anger was brought to light with his encounter with his brothers. His anger was the surface emotion of his true emotion of hurt. The truth brought him freedom in that he understood what God had planned yet he wrestled with his pain in being a part of God's plan. Joseph was second in command, married, had two sons, and lived a lavish life. Even with all of that, the truth was he was still hurt. Freedom came when he embraced his truth. What truth do you need to embrace?

# G.E.A.R.
## Giving Everything A Response

## Who Am I Becoming? FREEDOM

**Joseph's Reality**-Joseph had the power to torment his brothers. Joseph also had the power to embrace his truth that he was still angry. Freedom to walk out of bondade was his to do.

**My Reality**:_____
_____
_____
_____

**Joseph's Reflection**- Joseph made the choice to give into the lie that he was okay. In the heat of the moment he realized that he was still hurt and angry.

**My Reflection**:_____
_____
_____
_____

**Joseph's Responsibility**- It is more important to do the right thing in love than to be right in anger. The choice to extend grace and walk in integrity must be intentional.

**My Responsibility**:_____
_____
_____
_____

# Chapter Eleven

## Empowerment Shift #11
### FAILURE

*Strength can only be developed by effort and practice. As the physically weak man can make himself strong by careful and patient exercise, so the man with weak thoughts can become strong by training himself in thinking. To put away aimlessness and weakness and to begin to think with purpose is to enter the ranks of those strong ones who only recognize failure as one of the pathways to attainment. They make all conditions serve them. They think strongly, attempt fearlessly and accomplish masterfully.*

What is your greatest fear? What makes you cringe on the inside? Fear has way of holding us hostage. That which we fear is oftentimes the very thing we attempt to ignore. Fear of failure is on the top of the list for many men. Failure is falling over stumbling blocks that have the potential to be steppingstones. Failure is empowerment shift #11. Failure has the potential to be our greatest teacher if we allow it to be.

We develop strength through our struggles in life. Your thoughts about failure can release you to achieve greater or hold you hostage in the stuck place where you find yourself. Failure is a necessary part of life. When babies learn to walk, failure is their greatest teacher. Every time they fall, they learn. While they are not intentionally falling, it still develops their character and resilience. As you move from boyhood to manhood, failure comes with the movement. The how you perceive navigating the stumbling blocks of life will build your character as well as your resilience. You are the master of your thoughts. Your perception of why failure is necessary will ultimately take the fear out of the equation.

We do not subscribe to failure as a standard. We subscribe to failure as a non-threatening factor that happens as life happens. The goal is not to fail, however when we do, we pick ourselves up or allow others to help us up. Failure has its greatest impact when you use is as a teaching moment for ourselves as well as those who are watching us. There is always someone watching. You either teach them what they should do or what they should not do. Let's look at Joseph's story in Genesis 44:1-17 as we continue to explore the empowerment shift of failure:

And he commanded the steward of his house, saying, "Fill the men's sacks with food, as much as they can carry, and put each man's money in the mouth of his sack. ² Also put my cup, the silver cup, in the mouth of the sack of the youngest, and his grain money." So he did according to the word that Joseph had spoken. ³ As soon as the morning dawned, the men were sent away, they and their donkeys. ⁴ When they had gone out of the city, *and* were not *yet* far off, Joseph said to his steward, "Get up, follow the men; and when you overtake them, say to them, 'Why have you repaid evil for good? ⁵ *Is* not this *the one* from which my lord drinks, and with which he indeed practices divination? You have done evil in so doing.' ⁶ So he overtook them, and he spoke to them these same words. ⁷ And they said to him, "Why does my lord say these words? Far be it from us that your servants should do such a thing.

⁸ Look, we brought back to you from the land of Canaan the money which we found in the mouth of our sacks. How then could we steal silver or gold from your lord's house? ⁹ With whomever of your servants it is found, let him die, and we also will be my lord's slaves."¹⁰ And he said, "Now also *let* it *be* according to your words; he with whom it is found shall be my slave, and you shall be blameless." ¹¹ Then each man speedily let down his sack to the ground, and each opened his sack. ¹² So he searched. He began with the oldest and left off with the youngest; and the cup was found in Benjamin's sack. ¹³ Then they tore their clothes, and each man loaded his donkey and returned to the city.¹⁴ So Judah and his brothers came to Joseph's house, and he *was* still there; and they fell before him on the ground. ¹⁵ And Joseph said to them, "What deed *is* this you have done? Did you not know that such a man as I can certainly practice divination?"

¹⁶ Then Judah said, "What shall we say to my lord? What shall we speak? Or how shall we clear ourselves? God has found out the iniquity of your servants; here we are, my lord's slaves, both we and *he* also with whom the cup was found."¹⁷ But he said, "Far be it from me that I should do so; the man in whose hand the cup was found, he shall be my slave. And as for you, go up in peace to your father." ¹⁸ Then Judah came near to him and said: "O my lord, please let your servant speak a word in my lord's hearing, and do not let your anger burn against your servant; for you *are* even like Pharaoh. ¹⁹ My lord asked his servants, saying, 'Have you a father or a brother?' ²⁰ And we said to my lord, 'We have a father, an old man, and a child of *his* old age, *who is* young; his brother is dead, and he alone is left of his mother's children, and his father loves him.' ²¹ Then you said to your servants, 'Bring him down to me, that I may set my eyes on him.' ²² And we said to my lord, 'The lad cannot leave his father, for *if* he should leave his father, *his father* would die.' ²³ But you said to your servants, 'Unless your youngest brother comes down with you, you shall see my face no more.'

²⁴ "So it was, when we went up to your servant my father, that we told him the words of my lord. ²⁵ And our father said, 'Go back *and* buy us a little food.' ²⁶ But we said, 'We cannot go down; if our youngest brother is with us, then we will go down; for we may not see the man's face unless our youngest brother *is* with us.' ²⁷ Then your servant my father said to us, 'You know that my wife bore me two sons; ²⁸ and the one went out from me, and I said, "Surely he is torn to pieces"; and I have not seen him since. ²⁹ But if you take this one also from me, and calamity befalls him, you shall bring down my gray hair with sorrow to the grave.'

**30** "Now therefore, when I come to your servant my father, and the lad *is* not with us, since his life is bound up in the lad's life, **31** it will happen, when he sees that the lad *is* not *with us,* that he will die. So your servants will bring down the gray hair of your servant our father with sorrow to the grave. **32** For your servant became surety for the lad to my father, saying, 'If I do not bring him *back* to you, then I shall bear the blame before my father forever.' **33** Now therefore, please let your servant remain instead of the lad as a slave to my lord, and let the lad go up with his brothers. **34** For how shall I go up to my father if the lad *is* not with me, lest perhaps I see the evil that would come upon my father?"

Joseph failed his brothers. Joseph failed to be the man that God called him to be. He surrendered his will to wanting to get even with his brothers.. He lost sight of what God had intended for his life. The hurt that he felt led to an angry expression of a lie. Joseph fell over a potential steppingstone. Joseph's test revealed that he was not as strong as he thought he was.

Failure for Joseph was not rising above his impulse to make his brothers pay. Failure for Joseph was not calling on the spirit of God on the inside of him to help him manage himself in a more positive way. Joseph's strength rose as he continued his plot and God began to reveal his potential to have greater impact. His brothers were being tormented and God was not getting the glory out of that. Joseph eventually grabbed control of his thoughts which led to his strength being renewed. He surrendered his will to God's will for his life. The stumbling block became a stepping stone and God was able to use him in an impactful way. What stumbling blocks are potential steppingstones in your life?

# G.E.A.R.
## Giving Everything A Response

## Who Am I Becoming? FAILURE

**Joseph's Reality**-Joseph had his brothers right where he wanted them. He had the power to make them pay. Joseph failed his test.
**My Reality**:_____

_____

_____

_____

**Joseph's Reflection**- Joseph eventually came to himself. He eventually resisted his impulse to get even. In his moment of turning the stumbling block into a stepping stone he was forever changed.
**My Reflection**:_____

_____

_____

_____

**Joseph's Responsibility**- It is more important to do the right thing in love than to be right in anger. The choice to extend grace and walk in integrity must be intentional.

**My Responsibility**:_____

_____

_____

_____

# Chapter Twelve

## Empowerment Shift #12
## FEELINGS

*Feelings of doubt and fear never accomplish anything and always lead to failure. Purpose and energy are weakened when doubt and fear creep in. He who has concorded doubt and fear, has concorded failure. Thought allied fearlessly to purpose becomes a creative force.*

What makes you smile? What makes you cry? What moves you closer to God? What pushes you away from God? Feelings are unchartered territory. Men are taught not to cry. The narrative is that emotions are for women. If you feel you are a woman or acting like a woman. Merriam-Webster dictionary says that feelings (emotion) is a conscious mental reaction (such as anger or fear) subjectively experienced as strong feeling usually directed toward a specific object and typically accompanied by physiological and behavioral changes in the body. Feelings is empowerment shift #12. Our feelings are a direct result of what we think about any given situation in our life.

Our feelings are a valuable part of who we are as humans. Denying your feelings does not make you a man. Moving from boyhood to manhood requires you to be reflective in how you integrate your feelings into your daily life. Feelings of fear and doubt are going to come. When you connect your thought to your true purpose in God, your feelings will fall in line. When you attempt to dismiss them and minimize them, they will surface in various ways. Attempting not to feel is not an option. Feelings in and of themselves are not bad. Feelings are how we express who we are. The key to living an empowered and impactful like is controlling your feelings instead of them controlling you.

You decide how you feel. I know people say their feelings drive them. The truth is when you change your thought your feelings will follow. Let's look at Joseph's story in Genesis 45:1-4 as we continue to explore the empowerment shift of feelings:

> Then Joseph could not restrain himself before all those who stood by him, and he cried out, "Make everyone go out from me!" So no one stood with him while Joseph made himself known to his

brothers. [2] And he wept aloud, and the Egyptians and the house of Pharaoh heard *it.*[3] Then Joseph said to his brothers, "I *am* Joseph; does my father still live?" But his brothers could not answer him, for they were dismayed in his presence. [4] And Joseph said to his brothers, "Please come near to me." So they came near.

Joseph was overcome by his feelings. He could no longer contain himself, he had to let them out. How we manage our feelings is up to us. A hurt that has not been dealt with has no timeframe for healing. Joseph needed to be healed from the deep pain that he felt. His brothers betrayed him. The very people who were supposed to protect him put him in harms way because of their feelings. Joseph's life was full of struggles because of his brothers. His hurt from them did not destroy his love for them. Sometimes we get so consumed in our pain that we lose sight of what God is trying to do through us. What has your pain interfered with?

## G.E.A.R.
### Giving Everything A Response

## Who Am I Becoming? FEELINGS

**Joseph's Reality**- Joseph was hurting. Joseph gave into his feelings of anger for his brothers. He also gave in to his feelings of love for his brothers. The ones who were supposed to protect him put him in harms way.
**My Reality**:_____
_____
_____
_____

**Joseph's Reflection**- Joseph's feelings controlled him. In the moment he could not get control. It took God's love to move him from feelings of anger to feelings of love.
**My**
**Reflection**:_____
_____
_____
_____

**Joseph's Responsibility**- It is more important to do the right thing in love than to be right in anger. The choice to extend grace and walk in integrity must be intentional.

**My Responsibility**:_____
_____
_____
_____

# Chapter Thirteen

## Empowerment Shift #13
## FULFILL

*Individual responsibility must be absolute. A man's weakness and strength, wisdom and folly are his own and not another. A strong man cannot help a weaker man unless the weaker is willing to be helped. He must by his own efforts develop the strength which he admires in another, only he can alter his condition.*

What do you want out of life? What are your hopes and dreams? Where do you see yourself in 10 years, 5 years, next year? What are you doing to prepare for tomorrow? You are responsible for your life and how it turns out. God is not going to make you surrender. Fulfill is the mode through which you bring your destiny to pass. Fulfill is empowerment shift #13. Fulfilling your destiny is something that can only come through your intentional effort to make an impact.

You taking ownership of your life is the deciding factor in coming out better or bitter. Life has a way of handing us lemons, it is up to us to make lemonade. Your effort to develop you is a game changer. Your past does not dictate who you are destined to become. Your ability to develop other men going from boyhood to manhood is what achieving true manhood is all about. What good is it to attain all of this wisdom and not share it with the brother coming behind you. Reaching back is how you got to where you are. A man on his journey turned around to help you on your journey. That is how we fulfill our true destiny. Judging another man's journey is not helpful. Every man comes to the journey with their own load to carry. We do not know what it cost that man to get through his journey. What we do know is that God is available to help us all. God has a plan for all of us. It is up to us to yield our spirit to God's spirit. It is in the yielding that our true fulfillment will be revealed.

Life can be difficult. Life can be painful. Life can be unfair. Life can also be amazing. Life can be full of love. Life can also be full of joy that only God can supply. Let's look at Joseph's story in Genesis 45:4-28 as we continue to explore the empowerment shift of fulfill:

> Then he said: "I *am* Joseph your brother, whom you sold into Egypt. <sup>5</sup> But now, do not therefore be grieved

or angry with yourselves because you sold me here; for God sent me before you to preserve life. **⁶** For these two years the famine *has been* in the land, and *there are* still five years in which *there will be* neither plowing nor harvesting. **⁷** And God sent me before you to preserve a posterity for you in the earth, and to save your lives by a great deliverance. **⁸** So now *it was* not you *who* sent me here, but God; and He has made me a father to Pharaoh, and lord of all his house, and a ruler throughout all the land of Egypt.**⁹** "Hurry and go up to my father, and say to him, 'Thus says your son Joseph: "God has made me lord of all Egypt; come down to me, do not tarry. **¹⁰** You shall dwell in the land of Goshen, and you shall be near to me, you and your children, your children's children, your flocks and your herds, and all that you have. **¹¹** There I will provide for you, lest you and your household, and all that you have, come to poverty; for *there are* still five years of famine." '**¹²** "And behold, your eyes and the eyes of my brother Benjamin see that *it is* my mouth that speaks to you. **¹³** So you shall tell my father of all my glory in Egypt, and of all that you have seen; and you shall hurry and bring my father down here."

**¹⁴** Then he fell on his brother Benjamin's neck and wept, and Benjamin wept on his neck. **¹⁵** Moreover he kissed all his brothers and wept over them, and after that his brothers talked with him.**¹⁶** Now the report of it was heard in Pharaoh's house, saying, "Joseph's brothers have come." So it pleased Pharaoh and his servants well. **¹⁷** And Pharaoh said to Joseph, "Say to your brothers, 'Do this: Load your animals and depart; go to the land of Canaan. **¹⁸** Bring your father and your households and come to me; I will give you the best of the land of Egypt, and you will eat the fat of the land. **¹⁹** Now you are commanded— do this: Take carts out of the land of Egypt for your little ones and your wives; bring your father and come. **20** Also do not be concerned about your goods, for the best of all the land of Egypt *is* yours.'"**21** Then the sons of Israel did so; and Joseph gave them carts, according to the command of Pharaoh, and he gave them provisions for the journey. **22** He gave to all of them, to each man, changes of garments; but to Benjamin he gave him three hundred *pieces* of silver and five changes of garments. **23** And he sent to his father these things; ten donkeys loaded with the good things of Egypt, and ten female donkeys loaded with grain, bread, and food for his father for the journey. **24** So he sent his brothers away, and they departed; and he said to them, "See that you do not become troubled along the way."**25** Then they went up out of Egypt, and came to the land of Canaan to Jacob their father. **26** And they told him, saying, "Joseph *is* still alive, and he is governor over all the land of Egypt." And Jacob's heart stood still, because he did not believe them. **27** But when they told him all the words which Joseph had said to them, and when he saw the carts which Joseph had sent to carry him, the spirit of Jacob their father revived. **28** Then Israel said, "*It is* enough. Joseph my son *is* still alive. I will go and see him before I die."

Joseph's story at the end of his life was a reflection of the beginning of his life. He tended sheep. He cared for the vulnerable. After his father died, he could have turned on his brothers and his family. Instead he took responsibility for love. He did not take advantage of the weakness in his brothers. His brothers understood that they were wrong.

They knew that they did not deserve Joseph's grace. This shift is when you take responsibility for your yes to God to extend grace to the very people who are weaker than you. Here is where you accept that you cannot want better for someone who does not want better for themselves. Joseph's story is a lesson in how to have faith in God and focus on what God wants for your life. His story shows us how to be fertile ground for God to build our firm foundation. Joseph showed us what favor looks like and how fervent we must be in life. He taught us that being fruitful pleased God and having fervour honored God. We learned that our flow and freedom in God may lead to failure. In our failure we learn character and resilience. He taught us that honoring our feelings and changing our thoughts about who God called us to be will ultimately help us to fulfill our true destiny in God. My prayer is that this book has opened your eyes to who God has always known you could be. What do you see now?

## G.E.A.R.
## Giving Everything A Response

## Who Am I Becoming? FULFILL

**Joseph's Reality**- Joseph went through over 20 years of turmoil as a result of his brothers actions. He made the decision to honor God in order to fulfill what God always had intended for his life.

**My Reality**:_____

_____

_____

_____

**Joseph's Reflection**-Joseph trusted God when he could not trust himself. He was determined to honor God even when he was overcome with his pain and anger. He chose to say yes to God, he could not hold his brothers accountable for his yes to God.

**My Reflection**:_____

_____

_____

_____

**Joseph's Responsibility**- It is more important to do the right thing in love than to be right in anger. The choice to extend grace and walk in integrity must be intentional.

**My Responsibility**:_____

_____

_____

_____

Made in the USA
Middletown, DE
20 July 2023